# Alkaline Smoothies

*77 Delicious Alkaline*

*Diet Smoothies*

*to Balance your pH Levels*

Mark Oberstein

NORTHERN PRESS
PUBLISHING COMPANY

ISBN-13: 978-1548257286

ISBN-10: 1548257281

Published by Northern Press Inc.

# Let's Get Blending!

**It's long been known that eating a healthy diet abundant in fruits and vegetables are imperative to optimal overall health, including fighting diseases like cancer.**

The recipes laid out in this cookbook are very easy to make and for people on the go! Smoothies make eating healthy so much easier.  The absolute best advice you can get on eating healthy, alkaline focused smoothies is to focus on green, and also other colored foods that contain vital nutrients. Get your daily dose of green, red, yellow, orange and others because then you get the full spectrum of essential vitamins and minerals from your smoothies! So, let's get blending!

* Two quick tips for amazing smoothies: 1. Thicken with ice, if you put too much juice or other liquid ice thickens things up! 2. Start with the liquids, it makes the cleaning process much easier once you're finished.

## Fruit-Focused Smoothies

# Fruit Focused Alkaline Smoothies

# Banana Green Smoothie

1½ cups baby spinach

1 banana

1 cup frozen mango

Juice of 1 lemon

> Combine all ingredients into a blender and blend until fully smooth.

# Spinach, Grape, Coconut Smoothie

1 cup seedless green grapes

1 cup packed baby spinach

½ cup ice

¼ cup coconut milk

> Combine all ingredients into a blender and blend until fully smooth.

# Kale-Apple Smoothie

¾ kale chopped, ribs & stem removed

1 small stalk celery, chopped

½ banana

½ cup apple juice

1 tablespoon lemon juice

> Combine all ingredients into a blender and blend until fully smooth.

# Kale Pineapple Smoothie

½ cup coconut milk

1 ripe banana, chopped

2 cups stemmed and chopped kale

1 ½ cups pineapple, chopped

> Combine all ingredients into a blender and blend until fully smooth.

# Super fruit Smoothie

1 cup frozen cherries

1 kiwi, chopped and peeled

1 cup almond milk

1 tablespoon chia seeds

> Combine all ingredients into a blender and blend until fully smooth.

# Spinach, avocado, Apple Smoothie

1 ½ cups apple juice

2 cups spinach, chopped and stemmed

1 apple, peeled, cored and chopped

½ avocado, chopped

> Combine all ingredients into a blender and blend until fully smooth.

# Mango and Lime Green Smoothie

2 tablespoons lime juice

2 cups spinach, chopped and stemmed

1 ½ cups frozen mango

1 cup green grapes

> Combine all ingredients into a blender and blend until fully smooth.

# Pomegranate-Berry Smoothie

1 cup frozen mixed berries

½ cup vanilla low-fat yogurt

½ cup chilled pomegranate juice

> Combine all ingredients into a blender and blend until fully smooth.

# PB & J Smoothie

1 cup frozen strawberries

1 banana

¼ cup peanut butter

1 cup skim milk

2 tablespoons strawberries, chopped

> Combine all ingredients into a blender and blend until fully smooth.

# Razzle Dazzle Smoothie

1 cup frozen raspberries

½ cup frozen mango

½ cup pineapple

1 cup coconut water

> Combine all ingredients into a blender and blend until fully smooth.

# Sunshine Smoothie

½ cup frozen peaches

1 cup frozen strawberries

1 cup plain yogurt

1 strawberry

½ cup coconut water

> Combine all ingredients into a blender and blend until fully smooth.

# Piña Colada Smoothie

1 cup frozen pineapple

1 banana

1 cup coconut milk

1 tablespoon shredded coconut

> Combine all ingredients into a blender and blend until fully smooth.

# Banana Peanut Butter Smoothie

1 small banana

½ cup milk

1 teaspoon creamy peanut butter

3 ice cubes

> Combine all ingredients into a blender and blend until fully smooth.

# Hemp Protein Smoothie

1 cup hemp milk

1 scoop protein powder

¼ cup blueberries

¼ cup strawberries

½ medium frozen banana

3 medium dates

½ cup ice cubes

> Combine all ingredients into a blender and blend until fully smooth.

# Blackberry Apple Smoothie

2 cups frozen blackberries

½ cup apple cider

1 apple

2/3 cup non-fat lemon yogurt

> Combine all ingredients into a blender and blend until fully smooth.

# Minty Pear Smoothie

¼ honeydew

2 green pears, ripe

½ apple juice

1 cup ice cubes

½ cup fresh mint leaves

> Combine all ingredients into a blender and blend until fully smooth.

# Watermelon Smoothie

1 cup watermelon chunks

½ cup coconut water

1 ½ teaspoon lime juice

4 mint leaves

4 ice cubes

> Combine all ingredients into a blender and blend until fully smooth.

# Antioxidant Smoothie

1 Kiwi

½ cup pineapple cubes

1 banana

1 ¼ cup strong green tea

2 ice cubes

> Combine all ingredients into a blender and blend until fully smooth.

# Tropical Mango Smoothie

½ cup pineapple juice

1 cup diced mango

1 banana

2 teaspoons fresh lime juice

½ teaspoon ginger, peeled and grated

3 ice cubes

> Combine all ingredients into a blender and blend until fully smooth.

# Banana Almond Flax Smoothie

1 ripe frozen banana, diced in pieces

2/3 cup unsweetened almond milk

1/3 cup fat free plain Greek yogurt

1 ½ tablespoons almond butter

1 tablespoon flax seed meal

1 teaspoon honey

2-3 drops almond extract

> Combine all ingredients into a blender and blend until fully smooth.

# Mango and Lime Green Smoothie

2 tablespoons lime juice

2 cups spinach, chopped and stemmed

1 ½ cups frozen mango

1 cup green grapes

> Combine all ingredients into a blender and blend until fully smooth.

# Blueberry Protein Smoothie

¼ cup non-dairy milk

1 cup cold water

½ ripe avocado

½ cup frozen blueberries

1 scoop vanilla protein powder

> Combine all ingredients into a blender and blend until fully smooth.

# Orange Smoothie

1 orange, peeled

¼ cup Fat-free yogurt

2 tablespoons frozen orange juice concentrate

¼ teaspoon vanilla extract

4 ice cubes

> Combine all ingredients into a blender and blend until fully smooth.

# Banana Ginger Smoothie

1 banana, sliced

¾ cup vanilla yogurt

1 tablespoon honey

½ teaspoon ginger, grated

> Combine all ingredients into a blender and blend until fully smooth.

# Yummy Breakfast Smoothie

1 cup plain non-fat yogurt

1 banana

½ cup orange juice

6 frozen strawberries

> Combine all ingredients into a blender and blend until fully smooth.

# Blueberry Muffin Smoothie

½ cup low fat milk

4-6 ounces vanilla Greek yogurt

½ cup frozen blueberries

½ frozen banana

¼ cup raw, gluten-free oats

¼ teaspoon lemon zest

½ cup ice cubes

> Combine all ingredients into a blender and blend until fully smooth.

# Raspberry Green Tea Smoothie

1 cup green tea, chilled

1/3 cup plain non fat Greek yogurt

1 cup raspberries

1 large banana, frozen

1 tablespoon honey

½ teaspoon vanilla extract

½ cup ice

> Combine all ingredients into a blender and blend until fully smooth.

# Berry Green Smoothie

1 cup spinach leaves

½ cup frozen blueberries

1 ripe banana

½ cup milk

2 tablespoons old-fashioned oats

½ tablespoon sugar to taste

> Combine all ingredients into a blender and blend until fully smooth.

# Pineapple Passion Smoothie

1 cup low fat vanilla yogurt

6 ice cubes

1 cup pineapple chunks

> Combine all ingredients into a blender and blend until fully smooth.

# Tropical Papaya Smoothie

1 papaya cut into chunks

1 cup fat free plain yogurt

½ cup pineapple chunks

½ cup crushed ice

1 teaspoon coconut extract

1 teaspoon flaxseed

> Combine all ingredients into a blender and blend until fully smooth.

# Banana Blueberry Soy Smoothie

1 ¼ cups light soy milk

½ cup frozen blueberries

½ frozen banana, sliced

1 teaspoon vanilla extract

> Combine all ingredients into a blender and blend until fully smooth.

# Peach Smoothie

1 cup low fat milk

½ cup frozen peaches

½ cup frozen strawberries

2 tablespoons low fat vanilla yogurt

1/8 teaspoon powdered ginger

2 teaspoon whey protein powder

3 ice cubes

> Combine all ingredients into a blender and blend until fully smooth.

# Apricot Mango Smoothie

6 apricots, peeled, pitted and chopped

2 ripe mangos, peeled and chopped

1 cup reduced-fat milk

4 teaspoon lemon juice

¼ teaspoon vanilla extract

8 ice cubes

> Combine all ingredients into a blender and blend until fully smooth.

# Workout Energy Smoothie

1 ½ cups chopped strawberries

1 cup blueberries

½ cup raspberries

2 tablespoons honey

1 teaspoon lemon juice

½ cup ice cubes

> Combine all ingredients into a blender and blend until fully smooth.

# Sunrise Smoothie

1 banana

1 cup apricot nectar, chilled

1 container (8-ounces) low-fat peach yogurt

1 tablespoon frozen lemonade concentrate

½ cup club soda, chilled

> Combine all ingredients into a blender and blend until fully smooth.

# Berry Vanilla Smoothie

½ cup frozen unsweetened raspberries

½ cup frozen unsweetened strawberries

¾ cup unsweetened pineapple juice

1 cup fat-free vanilla yogurt

> Combine all ingredients into a blender and blend until fully smooth.

# Luscious Smoothie

1 cup skim milk

1 cup frozen, unsweetened strawberries

1 tablespoon organic flaxseed oil

1 tablespoon pumpkin seeds

> Combine all ingredients into a blender and blend until fully smooth.

# Slim Down Smoothie

1 cup frozen mixed berries

½ cup low-fat yogurt (any flavor)

½ cup orange juice

> Combine all ingredients into a blender and blend until fully smooth.

# Soyfully Good Smoothie

1 cup soy milk

½ cup frozen blueberries

½ cup corn flakes cereal

1 frozen banana, sliced

> Combine all ingredients into a blender and blend until fully smooth.

# Vegetable Focused Alkaline Smoothies

# Green Monster Smoothie

2 cups fresh spinach

1 banana

½ cup fat free plain yogurt

1 tablespoon peanut butter

1 cup fat free milk

1 cup ice cubes

> Combine all ingredients into a blender and blend until fully smooth.

# Spinach and Kale Smoothie

1 leaf kale

2 cups fresh spinach

1 cup almond milk

1 sliced frozen banana

> Combine all ingredients into a blender and blend until fully smooth.

# Broccolicious Smoothie

2 cups chopped broccoli

1 small cucumber, chopped

1 cup seedless grapes

1 lime, juiced

½ cup water

> Combine all ingredients into a blender and blend until fully smooth.

# Creamy Green Smoothie

½ medium zucchini cut in chunks

½ cup broccoli florets

2 small cooking apples, peeled, cored, thinly sliced

1 cup lime sherbet

¾ cup ice cubes

> Combine all ingredients into a blender and blend until fully smooth.

# Spring Green Smoothie

4 ounces fresh asparagus, trimmed and cut in 1-inch pieces (½ cup)

3 cups packaged baby spinach

2 ripe kiwifruits, peeled and chopped

½ cup white grape juice

1 cup seedless green grapes

¾ cups ice cubes

> Boil small amount of water in small saucepan and cook asparagus for 5 minutes, or until tender, then drain.

> Combine all ingredients into a blender and blend until fully smooth.

# Super Energy Smoothie

1 large handful spinach

1 cup cucumber, chopped

¼ jalapeno, chopped

1 small handful cilantro

2 sprigs mint

1 mango, chopped

1 cup coconut water

1 lime, juiced

> Combine all ingredients into a blender and blend until fully smooth.

# Electrifying Green Smoothie

4 leaves kale, stems removed

1 handful loose spinach

1 cup coconut water

4 fresh mint leaves

½ avocado

> Combine all ingredients into a blender and blend until fully smooth.

# Superfood Chia Smoothie

2 handfuls spinach

1 medium kale leaf

½ cucumber, sliced

2 tablespoons chia seeds

½ apple, cored, peeled, chopped

2 cups cold water

> Combine all ingredients into a blender and blend until fully smooth.

# Fat Burner Smoothie

3 broccoli florets

2 cauliflower florets

2 pineapple spears

Green tea to fill line

> Combine all ingredients into a blender and blend until fully smooth.

# Mean & Green Smoothie

2 stalks celery

1 cucumber

1 handful spinach

3 lettuce leaves

1 pear

1 lemon, juiced

> Combine all ingredients into a blender and blend until fully smooth.

# Super Detox Smoothie

2 celery stalks, chopped

1 small cucumber, chopped

2 kale leaves

1 handful spinach

1 apple, seeded, cored, chopped

2 tablespoons chia seeds

> Combine all ingredients into a blender and blend until fully smooth.

# Easy Spinach Smoothie

2 handful of baby spinach

1 cup low fat milk

1 small banana

> Combine all ingredients into a blender and blend until fully smooth.

# Heart Health Smoothie

½ cup packed flat-leaf, parsley (leaves and stems)

4 kale leaves (center ribs removed)

1 banana

1 cup frozen berries (an kind)

1 teaspoon ground flaxseed

> Combine all ingredients into a blender and blend until fully smooth.

# Kale Detox Smoothie

2 cups kale leaves, loosely packed

2 teaspoons ginger, grated

1 cup unsweetened almond milk

1 tablespoon chia seeds

1/8 teaspoon ground cinnamon

½ cup frozen blueberries

2 teaspoons raw honey

> Combine all ingredients into a blender and blend until fully smooth.

# Super Vibrant Smoothie

1 small cucumber

1 handful of spinach

Squeezed juice of 1 lime

1 tablespoon ginger, minced

1 apple, cored

1 cup water

> Combine all ingredients into a blender and blend until fully smooth.

# Veggie Smoothie

1 ½ cups tomato juice

¼ cup carrot juice

½ peeled cucumber

½ celery stalk

¼ cup each of parsley and spinach

½ cup ice

> Combine all ingredients into a blender and blend until fully smooth.

# Sweet Green Smoothie

1 small bunch broccoli florets (stalks removed)

1 teaspoon ground cinnamon

1 banana

1½ cups almond milk

1 tablespoon raw honey

> Combine all ingredients into a blender and blend until fully smooth.

# Cool Kale Green Smoothie

2 cups of kale

2 cups green grapes

1 cup ice cubes

> Combine all ingredients into a blender and blend until fully smooth.

# Mixed Alkaline Smoothies

# Sweet Honeydew and Mint Smoothie

½ honeydew melon (about 4 cups)

½ cup light coconut milk

1-2 fresh mint leaves

1 teaspoon lime juice

1 cup ice

> Combine all ingredients into a blender and blend until fully smooth.

# Blueberry Mint Smoothie

1 kiwi

2 cups frozen blueberries

3-4 large mint leaves

1 cup coconut water

2 cups spinach

1 cup ice

> Combine all ingredients into a blender and blend until fully smooth.

# Green Tea almond Smoothie

1 ½ cups strong green tea (cooled)

1/3 cup almonds

¼ cup raw honey

1 cup ice

> Combine all ingredients into a blender and blend until fully smooth

# Apple Spinach Smoothie

2 cups spinach

1 apple, chopped and peeled

½ cup silken tofu

¼ cup each orange juice and soy milk

1 tablespoon lemon juice

1 cup ice

> Combine all ingredients into a blender and blend until fully smooth.

# Mint Jalapeno Smoothie

1/3 cup fresh mint

1 jalapeno pepper, seeded

2 ½ tablespoons honey

2 cups plain yogurt

2 cups ice

> Combine all ingredients into a blender and blend until fully smooth.

# Carrot Glow Smoothie

2 large carrots, tops trimmed

1 granny smith apple, cut in quarters

1 naval orange, quartered and peeled

> Combine all ingredients into a blender and blend until fully smooth.

# Pomegranate cherry Smoothie

1 cup soy milk

½ cup frozen blueberries

½ cup corn flakes cereal

1 frozen banana, sliced

> Combine all ingredients into a blender and blend until fully smooth.

# Belly Buster Smoothie

3 medium apples

1 large cucumber

1 large lemon

1 lime

3 mandarins

1 head romaine lettuce

> Combine all ingredients into a blender and blend until fully smooth.

# Strawberry Mango Smoothie

1 mango, peeled and chopped

½ cup orange juice

2 tablespoons honey

10 strawberries cut in half

2 tablespoons lime juice

Ice cubes

> Combine all ingredients into a blender and blend until fully smooth.

# Root Juice Smoothie

1 medium beet, peeled and chopped

3 medium carrots, chopped

1 orange, seeds removed

½ lemon, seeds removed

2-inch piece turmeric root

1-inch piece fresh ginger

> Combine all ingredients into a blender and blend until fully smooth.

# Cucumber Refresher Smoothie

½ cucumber

2 limes, peeled

1½ cups coconut water

> Combine all ingredients into a blender and blend until fully smooth.

# Morning Smoothie

2 cucumbers

2 granny smith apples

1 large lemon, peeled

½ teaspoon ginger

> Combine all ingredients into a blender and blend until fully smooth.

# Immunity Smoothie

1 lb. Carrots

2 oranges, peeled

1 apple

Juice from ½ lemon

½ in. Ginger

4 sprigs of parsley

1 cup ice

1 tablespoon cinnamon

> Combine all ingredients into a blender and blend until fully smooth

# Apple, Beet, Carrot Smoothie

1 apple, cored and quartered

1 medium beet, trimmed, peeled, quartered

1 carrot, trimmed and peeled

> Combine all ingredients into a blender and blend until fully smooth.

# Cherry Orange Cranberry Smoothie

2 oranges, peeled

2 cups dark sweet cherries

2 fuji apples

2 tablespoons 100% cranberry juice

> Combine all ingredients into a blender and blend until fully smooth.

# Black Pepper Mango Smoothie

2 mangos, peeled and cored

4 carrots

Pinch of Black pepper and salt

1 Serrano chilli

> Combine all ingredients into a blender and blend until fully smooth.

# Minty Kale Smoothie

1 bunch of kale (14 leaves)

14 small mint leaves

¼ cup water

> Combine all ingredients into a blender and blend until fully smooth.

# Glow Smoothie

2 cucumbers, peeled

5-6 sprigs fresh basil

2 fresh mint leaves

Juice of 2 grapefruits

1 cup cold water

1 tablespoons coconut sugar

¼ cantaloupe

> Combine all ingredients into a blender and blend until fully smooth.

# Kale Craver Smoothie

3 cups kale

2 green apples

6 celery sticks

1 cucumber

1 garlic clove

1 tablespoon ginger

1 lemon

> Combine all ingredients into a blender and blend until fully smooth.

# Body Detox Smoothie

10 strawberries

½ lemon, peeled

10 stalks cilantro

1 ½ in. Ginger, peeled

½ cup water

> Combine all ingredients into a blender and blend until fully smooth

# WOULD YOU DO ME A FAVOR?

**Thank you for buying my book.** It is my hope that you have enjoyed the variety of recipes in this cookbook and that they aid you in your health

I have a small favor to ask. Would you take a minute to write a blurb on Amazon about this book? I look at all my reviews and love to receive feedback.

Visit the following URL to leave me a review:

## goo.gl/giQb1G

Also, if you have any friends or family that might enjoy this cookbook, spread the love and lend it to them!

Thank you, best wishes!

Paul

Made in the USA
Coppell, TX
26 December 2019

ISBN 9781548257286

9 781548 257286

# A Golden Adventure
## The Hunt for the Missing Rainbow

**Author:**
Sarah Beebe

**Illustrator:**
Sibghat